Be S

The Outloud Voice 4the Terminally Stupid

The Outloud Voice 4the Terminally Stupid

*A Dose of Insight for the Plague
that Infects Us All*

Alison E. P. Barr

Two Harbors Press

Two Harbors Press
212 3rd Avenue North, Suite 290
Minneapolis, MN 55401
612.455.2293
www.TwoHarborsPress.com

ISBN-13: 978-1-937293-24-6
LCCN: 2011936561

Distributed by Itasca Books

Cover Design and Typeset by Jill Kennedy

Printed in the United States of America

Contents

TERMINALLY STUPID PEOPLE

Acknowledgments

Thank you, to the amazing women in my
life that I'm blessed to call my friends.
They are always supportive and also honest
about the good, the bad, and the ugly.
Thank you, also, to my family, friends, and
husband who always support me.
This support makes dreams come true!

Foreword

Awareness!

That is what *Terminally Stupid* is all about!

We all need to be more aware!

More aware of how our actions affect others.

More aware of everyday things that we've forgotten.

More aware of the innocent, like children and animals.

More aware that speed and lack of attention can kill.

More aware that respect is the cornerstone to life in a
so-called civilized country.

More aware that we all deserve respect and in return
should give respect.

If we don't become more aware as our population
booms and our technology soars, the world will
become impossible to enjoy.

Be part of the solution, not the problem!

Introduction

If more than one person gives you this book anonymously—and highlights pages—then, congratulations, you are terminally stupid and people want you to know it!

This book is dedicated to all of the people that are sick of the rudeness and disrespect in the world today. It's directed inward at ourselves and outward at those around you. *When you think the guy running the stop sign is a jerk, ask yourself how many times you've done it.* It's also directed toward all of us who are in so much of a rush that we put lives at risk to make up that extra minute. All of the observations in this book are generalizations and opinions. Agree or disagree, that's your right!

TERMINALLY STUPID PEOPLE

On Community & Social Politics

We're all somebody's weirdo.
Get over yourself!

Most of us give ourselves that pat on the back for being a contributing member of society. Normal, balanced, "most people like us" kind of people. But just when your ego is getting too large for your head, you need to know that someone, maybe more than one someone, thinks you are a FREAK. Just remember that next time you're thinking about how great you are.

Litter

Seriously, anyone who still thinks it's okay to launch garbage out the car window, or drop it on the ground . . . terminally stupid!

- Is it supposed to be cool?
- Is it supposed to be an act of rebellion?
- Is it laziness?
- Is it the fear it will start to breed and multiply, so it must be disposed of immediately?

Really, the amount of garbage on roadways and in public areas is disgusting. In today's so-called environmental age it's inexcusable to litter. Wait until you get to a garbage can.

Cigarette Butts

Listen "butt" hole they are litter!

Cigarette smokers earn respect if they treat cigarette butts as litter. Put those butts safely in a proper receptacle. Nothing is more disgusting than going to a nice lake or walking path only to find cigarette butts everywhere.

If you want to poison yourself that's your business, but leave the environment and others out of your abuse. Plus, cigarettes start fires; tossing them out your car window can have serious repercussions. Grow up.

Social Stupidity!

Spitting on the sidewalk ...

Ewww, ewww, and ewww. If I need to explain or justify this choice, then you are terminally stupid! If you're walking with someone who does this, give 'em a good one in the back of the head. Disgusting! Keep your phlegm to yourself.

Picking your nose ...

Just remember, even though you're speeding down the highway, people can still see you picking your nose! Maybe just save that guilty pleasure for the bathroom; that way you aren't sharing the experience with all the other unwilling passengers in life.

Disclaimers

The cure is worse than the problem.

It may cure your runny nose, but it's likely to cause:

Heart attack

Stroke

Sight loss

Honestly, the average medication commercial spends 15 seconds on "what it will do to help you" and 45 seconds on what the serious and life-threatening side effects may be; the latter of which are rattled off at the speed of light.

If we put less crap in our bodies, we'd have less side effects to worry about. Try getting more sleep, reducing stress, eating healthy, and exercising; then see what medication you need.

Remember, pharmaceuticals are a multi-gazillion-dollar industry that masks problems and causes other problems.

Disclaimers in print . . .

Eyesight gets worse; fine print gets finer. Disclaimers should be in huge type or come with reading glasses. Isn't it ironic that the disclaimers get longer and more complicated, but our eyesight gets worse?

Clothing Restrictions

Clothing shouldn't just have size restrictions it should have weight restrictions.

Applauding a person's right to wear whatever they want is one thing but, seriously, if you have to lie down to zip up your pants think about buying a larger size. It's not pretty, it's not flattering, it's not honoring who you are; it's trying to be someone you're not.

Men's Speedos . . .

aka banana hammocks

aka budgie smugglers!

Ban them! Those men who have beautiful bodies don't often wear these. They go for baggy, cargo-type swimsuits. Many men who wear Speedos can't see them when they look down, and you can't see them on them. If you have to lift up a roll to pull them on, don't wear them. Not nice. Scars people for life.

The camel-toe . . .

Camel-toe is not attractive on anyone! Not sure what it is? Hold your fingers in a peace sign (the same shape as a cloven hoof, aka camel toe); now look at your crotch. If camel-toe is showing, your clothes are too tight. Your next appearance could be on "The People of Wal-Mart." Yikes.

The muffin-top . . .

Muffin-top is as difficult to ignore as camel-toe. Not nice, not flattering, not something to aspire to.

Farmers

No such thing as a happy farmer!

Most of us haven't seen or heard of a happy farmer. If they aren't complaining about too much moisture, then they're complaining that there isn't enough moisture; or that it costs too much to seed and they won't be able to sell the grain for enough to cover their costs. Never mind the plant/animal diseases, the herbicide and organic debates—the list is endless!

It's a tough gig, no doubt about it, but criticizing farmers is stupid; you're literally biting the hand that feeds you. They feed us and there are less and less of them all the time, and more and more people to feed. You do the math.

Support the farmers or tighten your belt. Unless you raise all your own food—which most of us don't— then support those who do raise the food, no matter how much they complain.

Dynamics

Doers vs. the slackers

Every office, every volunteer committee, every family, and every charity organization has the doers and the slackers. Too often the doers' hardworking ethics are tempered with the annoying martyr syndrome. These are the hardworking people that are attached to drama. After all, everyone needs to know they're doing all the work, right? Annoying.

Then there are the slackers. They actually do more work trying to look like they're working than actually doing work. The really annoying thing is that they think everyone else is too stupid to figure out that they're doing nothing. . . . NOT!

Dishes

The someone-else-will-do-it theory!

It can be men or women. For example, most of us have worked in a situation where there is a group kitchen where everyone is supposed to clean up after themselves. The furtive glance that accompanies quietly putting dishes in the sink, not allowing them to clank before casually exiting the kitchen, makes me want to deliver a serious bitch-slap. Knowing who it is makes it worse; co-workers are angry but afraid to comment. Yup, it's prevalent everywhere: someone else will do it. And these stupid people think that no one knows they are the ones leaving a mess for everyone else. BUSTED!

Email Etiquette

Learn how to BCC (blind carbon copy).

Congratulations, you have hundreds of friends that you forward emails to. NOBODY CARES! If you don't BCC, then you've now done the email version of telemarketing— you have given all these email addresses to spammers, sales companies, and sociopaths.

Take out the addresses before you forward messages. And don't, don't, don't REPLY ALL. There is nothing worse than getting hundreds of emails from people you don't know.

Public Toilet Seats

"If you sprinkle when you tinkle, be a sweetie and wipe the seatie."

It's an old rhyme, but remember it. If you're not going to sit down on a public toilet, fine. But wipe up after yourself. And make sure that you flush. If you have to wait for a minute before the toilet flushes properly, then wait. And if your young children use the cubicle, go in after them and make sure everything is as it should be. Why? Because everyone agrees that when you really have to go, there is nothing worse than going in and finding a toilet seat soaking, filled with whatever, and then having to walk out in search of a clean stall.

Movie theaters

Don't kick the seat, don't talk during the show!

What is it about people who are unaware of jiggling someone else's seat? Or people who are unaware of their children kicking the seat ahead of them? Nowadays with the cost of movies, nobody is going to sit there and have their enjoyment interrupted by seat kicking.

STOP IT!

And don't talk during the movie, just because you've seen it, or you have something you feel is IMPORTANT to say. Just zip it until after the show is done.

Vandalism

- Is for cowards!

- It's not cool!

- It's not something to be admired!

- It's terminally stupid!

- It's unproductive!

- It's costly!

- It's emotionally devastating!

- It's anonymous, so who the hell knows what the message is!

- It's destructive!

- It's illegal!

- Hopefully, somewhere in their future, acts of vandalism will come back to haunt the perpetrators, perhaps when they have families of their own.

- What goes around comes around!

Justice

The catch-and-release program sucks!

Countries that have dire consequences for crimes have very little crime to talk about. If you get your hands cut off for stealing, then you don't steal. If you get the death penalty for hurting someone, then you don't hurt people.

There is very little real fear of repercussions in North America. The courts are backed up, the prisons are full, and the most time-efficient solution is often a slap on the wrist and a dose of probation . . . until the next time, and there will be a next time. Why not? Crime does pay! Unfortunately, it demoralizes the enforcement agencies trying to make a difference.

"They"

Who the hell are they?

"You know, *they* say . . ." Who are *they*? Every intelligent, reasonable person in the world has used *they*—the unknown, mysterious *they*—to support a story or opinion. Are *they* experts? Are *they* the people next door? Are *they* real? Are *they* a figment of *our* imaginations? It seems as though *they* are the catch-all for trying to make the questionable credible. We should all make T-shirts that say, "I am they." How powerful would that make us?

Pot Smokers

Potheads don't think marijuana smells.

Truly one of the funniest things in life is the pothead. They are so out of it they think that pot doesn't smell. Most of us have caught a whiff of pot as we walked down a busy street and thought, *someone's smoking*. There's no smell like it. And that's how you KNOW someone is stoned. They'll say, "I don't smell anything. . . . Do you have anything to eat?"

If you smoke pot and don't want to get caught, go stand alone on a shore in a brisk wind blowing out to sea. It's the only way to do it without anyone knowing. TS (totally stupid). Truly, TS!

Celebrity Adultery

Guess what? The world is always watching. And adulterers will get caught.

Okay, celebrities choose a life in the spotlight. Or the life in the spotlight chooses them. Their picture is splashed all over—scratching their ass, sneezing, picking their nose—and people speculate what it all really means; yet these celebrities think they can get away with adultery. And they think that no one will ever talk about it.

There's no need to sum this up. These people are TS all the way. They typically get exactly what they deserve; unfortunately, the innocent also suffer. Shame on them! If there is something missing in their relationship then they should have the decency to end it.

Cover Your Ass

Lack of accountability.

Is anyone else sick of finger-pointing? Everyone is so scared of taking responsibility for things. It's like a hot potato; the last one holding it is to blame. Just once it would be refreshing to see someone get up on a talk show and say:

> "My parents were great.
>
> My childhood was awesome.
>
> School was a breeze.
>
> I'm just a turd."

Probably won't happen in this lifetime.

Emergencies

If you are told to get out-get out!

During every emergency, every disaster there are those that decide to "hold their ground" in some noble stupidity. But when the "fit hits the shan" it's rescue personnel that have to put their lives at risk to get these idiots out of the way. The cost of this should be directly on the idiots that decide to stay.

Emergency personnel would rather not be knocking on your door in the middle of the night risking their own lives. There is also a reason their engines are running, ready to get the hell out of there . . . because the situation is urgent. Take a hint and leave—fast.

If you decide to stay, write your driver's license number, with permanent marker, on your forearm and hold on for the ride. You might not have anything to live for but the people that have to save your butt do.

Rodeo

World's "toughest" sport.

Cowboys pay to ride livestock that weigh thousands of pounds and want to kill them. They are not paid hundreds of thousands of dollars to score a goal, hit a home run, or make a hole-in-one. They actually pay to climb on something that doesn't want them there. If they don't score, they go home broke. They ride with broken bones, torn muscles, and head injuries; if they break their riding arm, they switch hands.

When they go down, they usually get back up, or they're taken out on a backboard and they ride the next day. Rodeo truly is the toughest sport to make a living in. The risks are huge but cowboys and cowgirls do it because they love what they do and they have the hope of paying some bills.

To the rest of the world the rodeo might look like a *Terminally Stupid* way to earn a living, but these athletes deserve respect for their dangerous careers based on real-life ranch experiences still being used today.

TERMINALLY STUPID PEOPLE

On Vehicles & Pedestrians

Back to school
Driving, walking, or cycling should not be
contact sports.

These are not meant be death-defying activities. People need to take responsibility for staying current on the roles and rules for drivers, pedestrians, and cyclists.

Jaywalking

Remember, this is how gophers die!

If you're planning on crossing the road where you shouldn't, then don't interfere with traffic. The drivers don't have to stop! It would be nice if they were watching the road, paying attention just as you decide to launch yourself off the curb. But it's not your given right to jaywalk. Playing chicken with thousands of pounds of metal doesn't work well. If you get hit, it's an unfortunate accident but you are at fault. If you live you'll probably be featured in the Darwin Awards someday!

!

Tailgating

If you rear-end someone, you are at fault!

It doesn't matter why you rear-end someone, you will be at fault if you do. So why get up someone's butt? There is a three-second rule, in good weather, in good driving conditions. Pick a point along the road and once the car in front of you passes that point count to three; if you reach that same point before three seconds then BACK OFF! If the weather is bad, or road conditions are terrible, then double that time to six seconds. It's not rocket science, back off and avoid an accident. It's common sense.

Distracted Driving!

Cell phones, eating, drinking, etc., etc., etc.

Think about it. Many communities have implemented distracted driving legislation or they are drafting legislation to that effect. This is strongly supported by the insurance industry, as distracted driving plays a huge part in accidents. Realistically, it can't work without driver participation. In order to completely eliminate distracted driving, people would have to drive alone, with no music, no beverages or food, no purses, no animals, no children, no spouses, no shopping lists, etc.

What is more distracting than children in the vehicle? How about those who ride with an animal in their lap? What about when a spouse is talking in your ear? Nothing can spark a bad reaction like someone in the back saying, "I'm going to be sick." The distractions are really endless. People need to rely less on regulations and more on themselves. Drive by example for your children. Concentrate on what you're doing, and don't talk on the phone, don't let your children eat or drink when the vehicle is moving (to minimize choking or spills), and don't let them talk on the phone or text while the vehicle is in motion. Children learn by example, so set a good one.

Passing School Buses with Red Lights Flashing

Deadly!

Some cities and towns have put bylaws in place that overrule this traffic law, so school buses don't use them. But be aware, if a school bus has its red lights flashing then children will be crossing the street. School bus drivers and students are becoming more educated when it comes to pressing charges; all they need is the vehicle make, color, and license plate. Not that hard to get if the students are helping. Big money, big demerits. . . . The potential to kill someone—limitless!

Vehicles & Crosswalks

Don't be an impatient jerk!

Driving through a crosswalk while someone is using it means a big fine, big demerits. Edging up with your front bumper on the crosswalk and just waiting until pedestrians clear your car before you gun it is ridiculous. It's dangerous, stupid, and fineable. Do yourself a favor and review your basic driving manual.

All people need to do is pick up the phone and report the car's color, make/model, and license plate and the owner of the car is busted (yes, *the owner*, regardless of who was actually driving the car). This kind of behavior is a crime, putting lives at risk—shame on these *Terminally Stupid* drivers.

Bikes & Bike Riders!

Earn respect.

Bikes are vehicles. No they should not be ridden on crosswalks or sidewalks. Cyclists should not be riding side-by-side in a single lane either, and so on and so on. Yes, bike riders are supposed to stop at stop signs, signal for turns, and obey traffic signals. If bike riders obeyed more traffic rules they would garner more respect. It's a two-way street. Figure out which side to be on.

Drivers, give them some respect!

Passing cyclists when it's unsafe, not checking for bikes before opening doors, cutting them off, passing them on solid double lines . . . all of this is against the law, and often subject to the same fines as automobile-versus-automobile offenses. Grab a brain, cyclists have as many rights on the road as automobiles . . . they're just a lot more breakable!

Big Trucks

Just remember, 80,000 pounds goes into 3,500 pounds just once ... with nothing left over!

The next time you cut off a big truck or you get impatient with their speed or you pass them unsafely think carefully. How many times have you heard "collision with a semi" followed by news that the semi driver is fine but all members of the other vehicle were killed. Do the math! Big trucks don't stop quickly, maneuver quickly, or function quickly. But they do deliver practically every single product in your life—from the food you eat to the furniture that you sit on, it all arrived by truck. They keep countries running, so respect them.

Vehicle Lights

Most people flunked Mind Reading 101, so use the signal lights your car came with.

Talk about road rage. Wait at a stop sign for ten minutes for a break in traffic only to have the only break in traffic go whizzing by because some driver was turning and forgot to signal. Really, that's what they are for? . . . Who knew?

Daytime running lights don't run the taillights.

There's nothing more frustrating than driving in bad weather when nobody has turned on their vehicle's lights. The auto feature only turns on the front low-beam, running lights. This leaves your vehicle difficult to see from the back. "Auto" just means you can relax during the good times. So reach over and turn the lights on in bad weather. Most vehicles with an auto feature will also tell you if the lights are on when you turn the key off, so you won't forget to turn them off. Think about it, gray car, driving rain, no lights . . . Be smart enough to use your head for something other than resting a hat on.

Road Signs

Emergency personnel requested this one!

When rescue vehicles are parked across the road, with pylons on either side, the road is CLOSED! Don't edge up or get out of your car and walk up to the emergency personnel to ask if the road is closed. If it isn't, you'll be able to go forward. If the traffic isn't moving, well, then hopefully you have a good book. If you do get to edge past an accident then pay attention, because rubbernecking causes even more accidents. Be one of the smart ones and pay attention!

Questions not to ask peace officers and police personnel:

Don't you have something better to do?

Could you hold my beer?

Do you know this is the third time you've stopped me this week?

What's your problem?

Why are you picking on me?

I don't smell anything funny, do you?

Do you drink I've been thinking?

Don't you know this is a waste of taxpayer's money? Go and catch some criminals!

Traffic Tickets

Poor choices = personal stupidity

Tickets are the result of YOU breaking the law. Don't take your poor choices out on law enforcement personnel. On the contrary, remember these people when you hear a newscast that lists fatalities. Police, fire, and EMS deal with these realities every day so that WE don't have to.

Right on Red Light!

You still need to make a complete stop before proceeding!

This is NOT a blank check. If an area allows a right turn on a red light, you still need to stop and look both ways before proceeding. Rolling stops don't work! Red isn't just a pretty color. It means there are risks, so don't be *Terminally Stupid!*

Drinking & Driving

It's ridiculous this is in here but people STILL do it!

Go into a dark room, have no distractions. Sit there and think whether you can live with yourself if you were to drink and drive and kill a family of five. An accident is an accident. Drinking and driving is MURDER! Most drunks survive the accident; it's the other poor souls that don't.

Honestly, anyone who gets caught drinking and driving should have to spend a day with Mothers Against Drunk Driving (MADD) members who have lost loved ones. THAT would be a step toward justice.

Speeders

Congratulations, you got to the red light first!

Speed kills. You've got to be terminally stupid not to realize it. MOST of us are not properly trained to handle a speeding half-ton of steel if something goes wrong.

Is it really worth it to speed? You put your life at risk, your passenger's life at risk, and other drivers' lives at risk. Most accidents are caused by speed or inattention to detail. And, really, what have you gained except getting to the stop sign or the stoplight first? Yeah!

Drive the speed limit!

Driving too slow can be as dangerous as speeding.

Going too slow is a traffic offense and it is also dangerous, especially on two-lane highways. It causes impatience and frustration, which can result in bad decisions. Keep traffic moving at the posted speed.

Hey Einstein, here's a tip: If you don't have a valid license or registration—or you have warrants out for your arrest—don't speed.

Ask any traffic enforcement agent about this one. It is hysterical how many people with something to hide draw attention to themselves by speeding.

Guess what? If you drive responsibly, you probably won't draw any attention. But no- people with something to hide decide to speed. They'll probably be candidates for the Darwin Awards in the future, or have children just like them. Yippee!

Merging into Traffic

There are two pedals: gas and brake-use them!

Don't expect people to move over for you, slow down for you, or speed up for you. It's nice if they are able to, but it is YOUR responsibility to merge into traffic. Use your gas or your brake, but make a conscious decision to get it right. Get up to the speed of the traffic you're merging into and then make a decision.

Stunting!

Stupidity2

Roaring around town, excessive speed, donuts on ball diamonds, spinning tires! Here is the news. There are a very select group of individuals that can properly handle vehicles during these stunts. Young adults aren't amongst them. It's risky, hard on the vehicles, and dangerous to drivers, passengers, infrastructure, and other people on the road.

I'm not sure what is so attractive about this. Every town and city seems to have individuals that do this. Perhaps people could send in ads to the local paper with vehicle descriptions, license plates, and a list of the activities such drivers have been involved in. Let stunt men and women know they are being watched and recorded. Just an idea. Not sure what will work with this one. It's a dangerous, stupid, nuisance behavior that goes on and on.

Emergency Vehicles

Police, fire, or ambulance behind you or coming at you from the front? Pull over!

Get out of their way. There is nothing worse than pulling over, putting your hazards on because you have an emergency vehicle approaching, and then watching everyone pass you. They are getting in the way. Not cool.

The idea of everyone pulling to the shoulder is to create a lane down the middle so that emergency-response vehicles can get through. It's not rocket science. Pull over and STOP!

Double Solid Lines

Stupid, it means it's unsafe to pass.

Double solid lines are painted on roads when there is an unclear line of sight, an entry onto the road, or some other IMPORTANT reason.

A double solid line means "don't pass." Don't start to pass, don't finish passing. It means, "stay in your lane." Just for anyone too terminally stupid to figure it out still: DON'T PASS. Not even if you're on a crotch rocket that goes 300 mph and it will only take you 20 feet of that double line to get it done. Grab a brain. There's a lot of them not being used!

Crotch Rockets

Otherwise known as "donorcycles!"

Ever wonder why hospitals and organ transplant teams get excited when motorcycle season starts? It means there will be more organs to go around. These bikes that do 300 mph are nuts. Why are they built? Why they are allowed onto the streets is beyond understanding.

These maniacs weaving in and out of traffic at double the speed limit have passed everyone at some point. None of the tests they took to get that motorcycle license included controlling a bike at that speed. A small patch of gravel, a pothole, or a piece of debris on the highway and it's bye-bye. They are terrifying to watch and often mesmerizing, and often long gone after the accidents they cause. It doesn't make sense to make powerful machines like this for roadways. They should be outlawed or restricted to racetracks. It's just stupid.

Traffic Circles

aka roundabouts!

North Americans need to take a lesson. Literally, get on a computer and do some research. Signal lights are important, vehicle placement is important. Closing your eyes and gunning it is no way to treat a traffic circle. Some of them are two lanes, so it's even more important to know where to exit. Sometimes they are called "calming measures" for traffic control; in reality, they can cause anxiety in people who are not familiar with them. Get familiar with roundabouts. The information is out there, and they are becoming more and more prevalent.

Towing Trailers

When the tail wags the dog.

Don't listen to the salesperson when they tell you this minivan or SUV can tow an elephant. Go to a professional, like a commercial vehicle enforcement agent. Take your prospective vehicle specs—including tire size, wheelbase, and weight—and the specs of the trailer you want to tow.

Figure it out. There is nothing scarier than being passed by a vehicle towing a trailer that is whipping from side to side down the road. Basically, it is your responsibility to control the trailer, just like the dog controls the tail . . . not the other way around.

Sometimes the tow vehicle is so weighted down that the front end, which steers, has little contact with the ground. Add some speed to that and it's—yikes!— an accident waiting to happen.

Get some professional advice, and whenever you're towing a trailer SLOW DOWN. Also remember that you need more space when passing other vehicles before pulling back into your lane. Yikes!

TERMINALLY STUPID PEOPLE

On Family & Relationships

Communication and respect!
There is no guidebook or roadmap

Terminally Stupid people blame all their problems on someone else without ever looking at their own part in it.

"Any problem, big or small, within a family, always seems to start with bad communication. Someone isn't listening. " —Emma Thompson

Teenagers

Prepare your children!

Guess what! They are going to eventually leave home—if you're lucky. So, in their teenage years make sure:

- They do their own laundry
- Cook their own meals
- Budget their money
- Pay bills
- Make appointments
- Hold a job
- Deal with vehicle insurance (and pay for their own gas!)
- Know the importance of renter's insurance
- Clean up after themselves
- Make intelligent phone calls

You're not doing them any favors by doing everything for them. Get them prepared to be an adult!

Senior Citizens

Have patience; we'll all get there someday!

Seniors are the most relevant people in our society. Rather than get impatient with them, we should:

- Learn from them (they've already made their mistakes and learned from them)
- Respect them (they've earned it)
- Enjoy them (they've been der, dun dat)
- Celebrate them (they keep our politicians accountable)

They might drive a little slower, signal a little longer, hesitate for a moment or two . . . but, hey, they didn't live that long by being impulsive! Better to die from old age than be terminally stupid and die young!

Pirating

Just because you can doesn't make it right – it's theft!

Songs, movies, software, shows, and books are all subject to electronic theft. E-theft cheats those that put their heart and soul into these works. The artists who create them are cheated, the companies that invest their capital are cheated . . . it's theft. So spend the money if you appreciate the product; by doing so, you invest in the process. Anything else is criminal and terminally stupid!

OMG, LOL!

Great, even writing skills are being lost!

So we're raising a generation that doesn't know how to verbally communicate, and even writing skills are failing. Complete sentences are a thing of the past. And full words? . . . Lost. OMG, WTF, BFF, TTYL . . . Yup, communication in the future should be a riot.

Marriage

Isn't a word, it's a sentence . . . a life sentence.

And so it should be. Marriage rates are going down, divorce rates are going up; birthrates are going down, disease rates are going up. More marriages need to last a lifetime. Stupid people go into marriage with the exit already figured out. Having said that, there needs to be balance. If you're not happy in a marriage then show some respect and end it before you commit adultery.

Pajamas

Keep the pajamas in the bedroom, please.

Pajamas are supposed to be for nighttime. Only your family should see you in them. What do you suppose your co-workers think of you when you wear pajamas with cute kittens on them into the office? Guess what? It's not "new fashion," it's not "hip;" it's lazy. Did you wear a suit to bed and get confused? Really, pajamas are meant to be cozy, loose, comfortable . . . but not in the office building, not in the shopping mall, and not in a restaurant. Keep them for the bedroom.

TV Remotes

Just because you can switch channels ... don't.

There is nothing more frustrating than trying to sit with someone watching several channels. If you're alone, feel free, switch away! If you are sitting with someone else then pick a friggen' channel and leave it. Click, click, click . . . grrr–.

Body Piercing

Why not just admit you like pain!

It's not about making a rebellious statement.

It's not about looking cool.

It's not about feeling good or fitting in.

Admit that some part of you likes pain.

It certainly doesn't look cool, it doesn't sound cool. There is nothing cool about trying to figure out what some kid is trying to say while lisping around his tongue piercing. Again, ask yourself *why* you want to put your body into shock this way. Every hole in your body will continuously try to heal. When you pierce yourself, your body is saying, "DANGER, DANGER!" It certainly isn't attractive. Some very beautiful people, inside and out, go overboard and pierce their body all over. Why? It isn't pretty.

Money

Learn the value of a dollar.

Many kids these days have no concept of the value of money. Probably every generation has said that so, perhaps, there is hope. Once kids are teenagers they should be capable of earning money. Extra chores around the house is a good way for teens to earn money; then when they want something, some of their money goes to pay for it.

It's not that difficult, but so many parents don't teach their children to budget, to save for what they want, to make a conscious decision before they purchase something. Take a moment to add up all the household bills. If your children have no concept of what it takes to run a household, spend some time teaching them. Someday they'll need to earn it themselves.

Hoodies

aka (for oldies) Kangaroo Jackets.

Look up and live! Peripheral vision can save your life! Honestly. Is it really cool to slouch around, hiding in your hoodie? You can't see, you can't hear, and it doesn't look cool; it looks like you don't have much to live for. Making eye contact, experiencing the world around you is where the future lies. Get on with it! Otherwise, launch yourself into traffic without making eye contact, even on a marked crosswalk. Go ahead, become a hood ornament.

Customer Service

Raise your kids to make eye contact!

Going into any business and having a young kid mumble something while looking down at their cash register is just plain frustrating. So is saying hello to a young adult out walking, biking, or skateboarding only to get nothing in return. Making eye contact will give them a leg up in the world. Social skills are important!

Children

The greatest gift you can give your kids is your time!

That ultimate snowboard or jacket or iPod will quickly be forgotten as something better comes along. The kids that make something of themselves are not the ones that have received every material gift in the world. It is the kids that spend quality time with their parents, experiencing the ups and downs of life, learning to communicate, and dealing with life's tough issues that succeed. Stop compensating and start participating!

Speak Out

Good or bad.

If you've been to a restaurant and you've had exceptional service then let the manager know who it was and how they were exceptional. If you've had bad service don't just bitch about it and never go back, let the manager know so they can make changes. If the manager doesn't seem to care then DON'T GO BACK! How are things supposed to change if nobody knows!

Our Bodies!

We don't drink poison ... we do it slowly!

As far as we know we only get one body! So everything you eat, drink, inhale, put on your skin, clean your house with, etc., gets processed by your body, specifically your liver! The incidents of cancer are growing. Processed food, cleaning products, and personal care products are all filled with chemicals that don't help. A good rule of thumb is if you can't pronounce something then don't use it or ingest it. Go natural as much as possible. It sustains our health, our planet, and our future.

Courtesy

Be courteous!

Even if you're at a marked crosswalk and someone stops for you, a smile and wave can go a long way. Acknowledge the gesture. Courtesy is a lost art but it can brighten a day. Reward and acknowledge good service and extra effort. Remember the basics: thank you, please, a pleasant tone. People aren't born with people skills but it is a valuable asset! Be sure to use all five fingers when you wave—not just the middle one!

Verbal Communication

There is a "lost" generation coming!

Whether we like it or not the next generation is capable of mastering every gadget out there but this has cut out the art of verbal communication. Many kids aren't capable of having a spoken conversation. They can communicate by way of texts, Twitter, Facebook, video games, iPhones, iPods, computers, and many other electronic devices, but can they "talk" to you? Teach your children to communicate before it's a lost art!

Screaming Children

Nothing about this is acceptable!

Why should your child be allowed to throw a tantrum or yell and scream in a public place? Adults aren't allowed to behave like that, so why should children? There is nothing more distracting and annoying than seeing some child throwing a fit in a restaurant, grocery store, or some other public place. Such behavior shows a lack of control by the parents. Just because the parents are used to it and ignore it doesn't mean the rest of the world should have to deal with it. Haul those kids' butts out of there. Pronto!

Not Paying Attention

Children are put on Ritalin for not paying attention—why not adults?

Talking to someone who is texting, dealing with someone who hasn't read the entire email, talking to someone who then takes a cell phone call . . . and it's the children that are given drugs? Stupid, stupid, stupid.

Lead by example: pay attention to people when you're with them, read emails completely, and finish a conversation properly. Teach your children how to focus, and how to finish things. Or, perhaps we should have Ritalin vending machines at work; then we'd all have better attention spans.

Stressed

Desserts spelled backwards!

Stress is what we make of it—good or bad. It can motivate, it can cripple. We subconsciously let it run our lives in a way it never has in generations past.

Adults, ask yourself how many sports you were able to play as a teen. Probably a lot less than you have your children enrolled in. Ask yourself what your debt load is; ask yourself when you last gave yourself one hour to do whatever you wanted.

Stress can be one of the most poisonous things out there. It's blamed for causing everything from tardiness to murder! But the only one who gives it power is YOU!

Patience

Usually the first thing to get lost!

More minor mishaps escalate because someone chooses to lose their patience. It is a choice. Sometimes it isn't a conscious choice but it is a choice. Take a moment, take a deep breath, ask yourself what the problem really is and then try to deal with the situation. Flying off the handle does more harm than good. There is nothing worse than reliving an incident again, and again, and again, knowing that you could have handled it better. Yuck!

Cell Phone Etiquette

Pay attention.

If you're in a public place, talking to someone, speaking to your spouse, or eating a meal, don't answer your cell phone. Don't make a call, and don't text with one hand while trying to carry on an intelligent conversation because it won't work. Don't be terminally stupid and do any of these things while you're behind the wheel or you really will wind up as a statistic . . . worse, you could take others down with you.

TERMINALLY STUPID PEOPLE

On Business & Politics

Apathy isn't an excuse it's an epidemic
Educate yourself, get involved and informed.

People have no excuse these days for being apathetic about what's going on around them. There are so many ways to get informed about politics, home buying, children's education, foreign policies, and so much more without leaving the comfort of your own home.

Soldiers

If you're not behind them then stand in front of them!

Don't take your opinions and political views out on them. They do the job they are trained and told to do. They literally put their lives on the line so that people can have an opinion and be free to express it. Make sure you support any decision that makes sure these men and women get the best equipment and all the support they possibly can. Whether you agree with the mission or not is irrelevant. They protect and serve so you can sleep safely at night.

Animal Testing

It's cruel and inhumane.

Those that argue that "they are just animals so it doesn't matter" or that "animals don't feel pain" should walk a mile in their shoes. If this is your opinion then spray hairspray directly into your eyes and see how it feels. Don't support personal care products or cleaning products that don't specifically state "not tested on animals." Animals have different pain levels than humans but they feel pain and they suffer, often silently.

Anyone who thinks differently is terminally stupid and will hopefully come back in their next life as an animal that is in a test facility.

Toxic People

We all know them.

Everything that comes out of their mouths is negative. Nothing is ever good in their lives. Recognize it and cut it out of your life. This energy can suck the life right out of you. Don't let them. It's TS to let someone take you down with them.

Voting

Get out and vote!

Men and women have died in the past for the right to vote. Men and women still die in some countries for the right to vote. Most North Americans treat it like the plague; they can't be bothered to get out of their chair, put in a little bit of effort to get out and vote. Take some time out of your TV schedule and learn what the issues are and then get out and vote. Teach your children the necessity of getting out to vote when they qualify. North America has the lowest percentage of people that get out to vote and yet they are the first ones to bitch about the ones that get into power. Get off the couch and get out and vote!

Citidiot!

Look around before you move out to the country!

The feedlot was there before you moved in, the neighbors had livestock before you moved in, and the neighbors had a kennel before you moved in. Look around BEFORE you move. There are realities in the country that you may be moving into. Don't expect to make changes after you've moved or you'll become the whiner that nobody can stand. If you left the city to get away from the hustle and bustle, here's some reality!

· No one will be around to pick up your garbage, unless you pay them.

· No one is going to plow your driveway, unless you pay them.

· Living in the country doesn't mean your animals can run around and "be free." They are not welcome on other people's property.

· Livestock and farm machinery use the roadways, so you'd better be patient or you'll get a taste of rural justice, such as letting that herd of cattle take the long way home.

· The nickname for inconsiderate people that move to the country is "citidiots" . . . don't be one!

Educate Yourself on Development

A developer's goal is to make money!

It's hard to believe but developers think in dollar signs. Many are ethical and have long-term sustainable goals. Others just build the communities and then move on. Beware! Look at everything before you buy. Ask the municipality what is going in beside you, what is already there, where the flood plains are, and what the long-term development plans are in the area. Be aware of the promises for the future, get it in writing, seek legal advice on the contract, and check the reputation of the developer. Buyers beware!

Airlines

Motto: We're not happy until you're unhappy!

Tighter security, less luggage, higher prices . . . but fewer guarantees. People are screened but luggage isn't. Where is the logic in that? There are extra charges for too many bags and still no guarantees they won't lose them. There is increased taxation to cover increased security measures and still no guarantees. You have to arrive earlier for flights but receive no guarantee that flights won't be late. Seems pretty one-sided, huh? What a good incentive to drive.

Airplane seats . . .

Just because they go back doesn't mean they should. Respect on airplanes should be doubled. There is nothing worse than having food sitting on the tray when somebody ahead of you slams the seat back. Be courteous, take a look, see if it will bother someone before you stuff the back of your seat in their nose. Airlines are out to make money so they provide less space on their planes. If everyone takes a moment to be considerate, it can improve the experience for all airline passengers.

Dentists

Don't ask questions.

Jeez, I think it must be the school of torture that these sadists go to. Not only do they have your mouth propped open, sticking needles into it but they are talking . . . and asking questions! What the hell are you supposed to do? It's nasty when they are on a topic that incites a passionate response, yet you have to keep your mouth propped open. Grrr– by the time the gadgets are out of your mouth the moment has passed. Personally, I think they do it on purpose. Maybe it's a little payback for one of the most hated professions, next to proctologists.

Shop Locally

Save time and fuel while supporting your local economy!

It's a win-win situation, but in return the retailers need to be within the ballpark on their prices. Try to get your car service, groceries, hardware, etc., in your own community. Support those businesses that in turn support the community. Be current on your facts. Your "local" co-op may actually be an international franchise, but that particular store may be owned and operated by someone local. A healthy community supports itself.

Cultivate the locals . . .

Businesses that survive cater to the locals! If your business is in a tourist town then the reality is that tourism ebbs and flows with the season and the economy. During busy times it's easy to forget that locals will keep businesses going through the lean months. It's also locals that spread the word about businesses . . . good and bad! So make sure to cultivate the locals, offering specials that will bring them in the door and have them promoting your business. If you price to the highest, or tourist, levels the locals will back off.

Telemarketing

Torture to the companies!

It's not the person dialing the number that is responsible; they're just doing a job. But the companies . . . hmm . . . How to get back at the companies that support this? More importantly, how to get them to stop! I have no answer for this one, but it is fun to toy with the telemarketers sometimes. Favorite comeback lines:

"Can I have your home number? I'll call you back while you're having supper."

"No . . . they never found the body."

Be original, not abusive.

Outsourcing

If you don't support companies outsourcing to low-income countries, don't use or wear their products.

There is nothing more hypocritical than criticizing outsourcing and then wearing all products "Made in China" or "Made in India." Many, not all, of the workers in these countries are exploited; they are paid very little and work in deplorable conditions. Outsourcing saves the manufacturer money but this is not necessarily passed on to the consumer.

It also takes jobs away from the local economy. Be aware, ask questions, read labels, and check the Internet to find out where products are made and by whom. Find out whether the company pays a fair wage, and how the product is actually made, such as the manufacturing process and ethics. If it isn't ethical then don't support it.

The Media

Don't shoot the messenger!

We all love to curse the insensitivity of the media when they stick their microphones in grief-stricken faces, but remember the public wants to know what's going on! It is not easy asking the tough question and most of the time they are also the obvious and painful questions. But the public wants to know, that's what drives newspapers, news shows, magazines, and various other media.

It's the morbid curiosity that most of us are born with. Just remember, these people have families, too; and, in their own way, they do the job to make a difference. If you don't like their technique then don't buy their product.

Weathermen or meteorologists . . .

Where else can you be consistently wrong and keep your job? There's nothing like having shorts on and winding up in a snowstorm. Think about it . . . if most of us got our jobs wrong as often as weathermen do, we'd be out of a job. And they go to school to be that wrong. They get a fancy title and they're still wrong! Sounds like a great gig if you can get it; almost like being a politician.

Weather Forecasts

Give your news people a window! There is nothing that undermines the credibility of the media like a totally wrong weather forecast. To say there is a "slight chance of rain" when it's dumping buckets outside makes people roll their eyes and change the channel. If nothing else, get someone to check outside right before the broadcast. Radio stations are really bad for this. They read the morning forecast in the evening and it's ALL WRONG. Doesn't someone have a window to check? Credibility!

Politicians

Remember they can promise whatever they want until they get into power!

None of the inaugural politicians are privy to the secrets of the office until they are elected. They might promise to lower the cost of living or pull out of a war but until they get into the office and find out what deals were made, what is really at stake (which most of us will never know), then it's all just empty promises. You'll notice that incumbent politicians are more careful about what they promise. Pick the politician that makes realistic statements. They're hard to find, but they are out there.

Medical Advice

Fight for yourself.

It's no secret: medical professionals are overworked and taking shortcuts. They are not gods; they don't have all the answers. Individuals need to fight for themselves.

Ask questions. Be informed. Some people go to the same doctor for decades and are happy like that. But does that doctor *listen* after two decades or do they have a diagnosis before you even walk in the door.

If you feel there is a test that needs to be done or if you feel there is something more going on, then make it known; go to a walk-in clinic or emergency room for a second opinion—or get in your doctor's face and make demands. You have a voice. Use it! If you don't fight for yourself no one else can!

Citizenship

If you left your country because you wanted a better life—you were oppressed, abused, threatened, or in fear for your life—then adopt the customs of the country you run to! None of us can go to oppressed countries and expect to carry on with North American customs. We'd wind up dead. Be loyal to your adopted country first or that country will become like the one you escaped from.

Many people "escape" to have a better life . . . so welcome! But be loyal. The right to a voice is the greatest asset but these rights are based on equality . . . as in everyone is equal. If you don't like it, then go back to your own country—and good luck.

Bosses

Remember, a bad boss can only affect you while you're at work, your personal life is off-limits, so keep things in perspective and don't give them the power to ruin even an hour of your life!

Almost everyone has had a boss with no people skills, no management skills, less experience than everyone else on staff, or all of the above and then some. They should treat everyone with respect. That's how they earn respect. Being your friend isn't part of their job description but they should be the one you turn to when there is an issue—good or bad—with work! Don't let them bully you or intimidate you. No job is worth that.

Remember, they put on their pants one leg at a time just like you do. And if YOU are the boss, think about these things. There are courses to help you figure these things out. You don't want to be the type of boss that causes people to cheer and do a tap dance of joy when they find out you're going on vacation do you?

TERMINALLY STUPID PEOPLE

On Animals

Excuses are easier to come by than solutions. Manners and respect apply to animals and humans.

When it comes to people and animals it's easier to ignore a problem until it becomes unmanageable. Poor behavior should have consequences no matter what the species. It's not normal or natural for people or animals to act badly; it's usually a sign of frustration and confusion. Be part of the solution and ask for help if you can't fix it by yourself.

Pets

Remember, animals are innocent and dependent ... they are not disposable!

Animals have animal needs and animal instincts. Misbehavior is often a sign that their needs are not being fulfilled. We see it as "bad behavior" when in reality it is a sign of their frustration. Once animals manifest this undesired behavior (some of it may be instinctual behavior) many owners decide to get rid of the problem instead of dealing with it. Shelters are full of animals that people didn't commit to. Consult a professional trainer or access the myriad of resources out there—the TV, the net, books, CDs.

Pets require structure and discipline they can understand, just like children. Calm, consistent correction will produce desirable results. There needs to be understandable consequences for bad behavior. Ironically, most of the time it's the owner's issues causing misbehavior, not the animal's issues. Animals have so many positive things to teach humans. Amongst these traits is the fact that they live in the moment and don't hold grudges. We should all learn from them.

Horseback Riding Etiquette

Safety is more important than showing off!

If you're out riding in a group, ride to the ability of the most inexperienced rider. Don't expect them to come up to your level. Don't change speeds before asking the other riders. When coming to an obstacle, road, or creek, check that everyone is safely across before riding off; horses have herd instincts and can panic if left behind.

More citidiots . . .

Don't honk your horn when passing livestock or people horseback riding! News release: animals are unpredictable and instinctual. They can be easily startled so don't honk your horn, even if it's just to acknowledge someone you know. Many riders don't have a problem with it, but it only takes one startled horse to cause a chain reaction. Welcome to the countryside, when around animals it's common to move slowly and smoothly, drive the speed limit, and get along with the locals. Don't be a citidiot!

Dogs vs. Children

Small children with large dogs on a leash!

It doesn't matter how calm or quiet the dog is. If a squirrel runs across the road, it is a recipe for disaster. Dogs have strong instincts to chase, to defend, and to run. Children don't have the reflexes to deal with this situation so they will likely be pulled down the street and, ultimately, hurt. Use common sense: let the child hold the leash WITH you but do not let the child take control of the animal.

Dog Tags

Dog's name and owner's phone number!

Dogs are instinctual. The shelters are full of dogs that would "never run away" and then they do. They run to chase something, they run in fear of something. It's their nature. Dog registration or rabies tags typically don't have phone numbers on them. If you pick up a dog during work hours and contact the municipality on the tag, someone may take the time to try and contact the owner but they cannot give you this information. If you find a dog outside of office hours, they will probably be shelter-bound.

It's so easy to get a tag with the dog's name and your cell phone number. It saves time, heartache, resources, and lives. Many people that move to the country claim they don't want the dog to get hung up on something and choke to death; they want them to be "free." There aren't many reports about canine skeletons hung up on things. It's far more likely that a vehicle will hit them.

Dog Crap!

If you won't let your kid crap on someone else's lawn then why let your dog!

Pick up after your pet in all public places. It's all too common to see a dog taking a crap on someone's lawn while the person on the other end of the leash looks around to see if anyone is witnessing the dirty deed. It's offensive. Carry a bag and pick up after your dog. And teach your kids to do the same when they are walking the dog. Responsible pet owners make responsible parents. Think about that next time you walk away from a steaming pile of shit!

Aggressive Dogs

They weren't born that way!

No matter what the breed of dog, they are not born aggressive. People make dogs vicious and neurotic. If someone has an aggressive animal, look very closely at the people that own that dog. That's where it comes from.

A very good way to learn what someone is really like is to take a look at how the family pet behaves. Are they hyper, overly energetic, cowering, timid, dominating, aggressive, noisy, overly spoiled, etc., etc.? People make them this way. Often the pets are a reflection of their owners. Not in looks but in manner. Look closely at how they treat their pets. Do they yell, dominate, degrade, coddle, baby, ignore, dismiss? . . . This will give you a valuable look at the person within!

Dogs react to your energy. Yelling at your dog translates into excited energy and that is all that your dog understands, that you're excited for some reason. For example, if they poop on the floor and you yell at them, they will likely think their excitement is justified because now you're excited, too. Yay!

Dog Bites

Remember, dogs only bite for two reasons, because they feel they have to and because they can. In the dog world, biting is a form of communication, so it's up to the owners to give them the direction that this is not acceptable.

Dog Etiquette

Have control or keep them on a leash!

Control your dog. If your dog consistently comes when called in ANY situation then let them be free. However, if someone else is approaching, with or without a dog, the proper thing to do is recall your dog and leash him or her. Yelling, "he's friendly," as your dog ignores you and runs toward someone who is deathly afraid of dogs, or is trying to control two large dogs on leashes, is unacceptable.

Inconsiderate dog owners are making it harder and harder for responsible dog owners. If your dog doesn't consistently listen to your commands, then you are putting your dog's life and possibly others lives at risk. Call a trainer. You spend thousands on your kids, so why not spend money on your dog? You'll both enjoy a better life.

ABOUT THE AUTHOR

After witnessing one too many examples of the decline of social courtesy, Alison declared war on rudeness and stupidity. Some might think this fight is a lost cause, but Alison holds out hope, hope that all people need is a gentle reminder to pay attention to what they're doing.

Alison's goal is that this book will give people a voice and a tool to use when they want to tell someone they are terminally stupid! She also hopes that it will give people something to think about when they are acting terminally stupid themselves.

⟶꙰꙰⟵

Find more inspiration on her website:

www.terminally-stupid.com